HOSIE'S ALPHABET

HOSIE'S ALPHABET · PICTVRES BY
LEONARD BASKIN · WORDS BY HOSEA
TOBIAS & LISA BASKIN · THE VIKING PRESS ·

Copyright 1972 in all countries of the International Copyright Union by
Leonard Baskin. All rights reserved. First published in 1972 by The Viking
Press, Inc., 625 Madison Avenue, New York, N. Y. 10022. Published
simultaneously in Canada by The Macmillan Company of Canada Limited.
Library of Congress catalog card number: 76-109716

Pic Bk   1. Alphabet books

SBN 670-37958-1

Printed in Japan   Bound in U.S.A.

HOSIE'S ALPHABET

A The armadillo, belted & amazonian

B

Bumptious Baboon

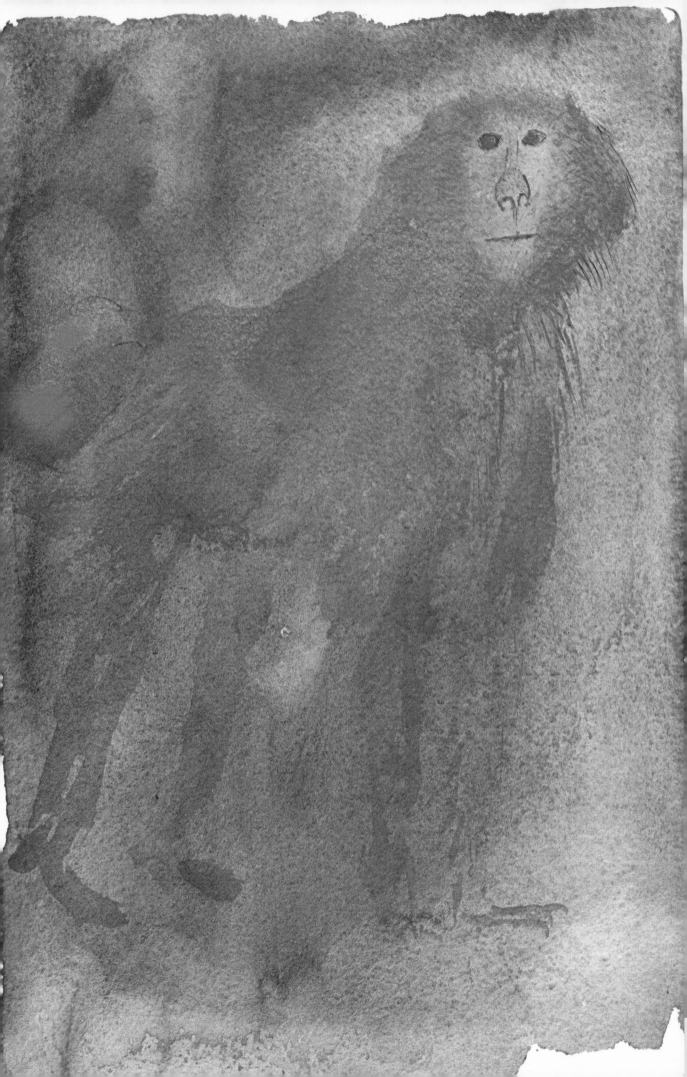

C *The carrion crow*

D
is
for
demon

E *The imperious*   *eagle*

spangled and splendid

F   A furious fly

G

A ghastly

garrulous

gargoyle

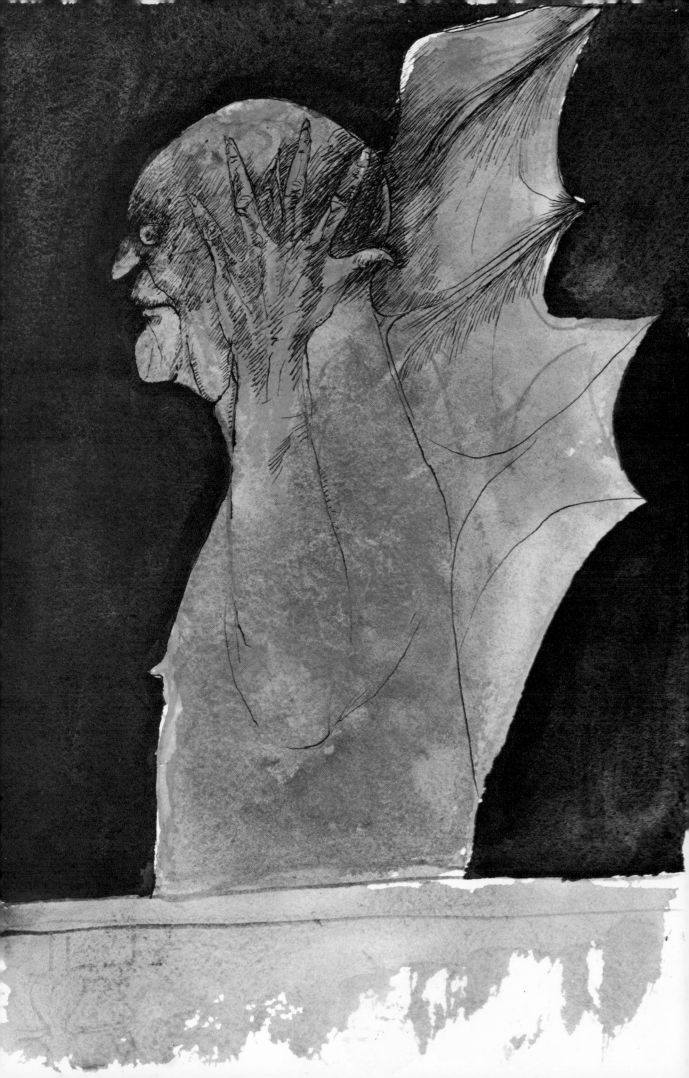

H   Hosie's heron

I
An incredibly scaly iguana

J

The electrical jellyfish

K *A quasi kiwi*

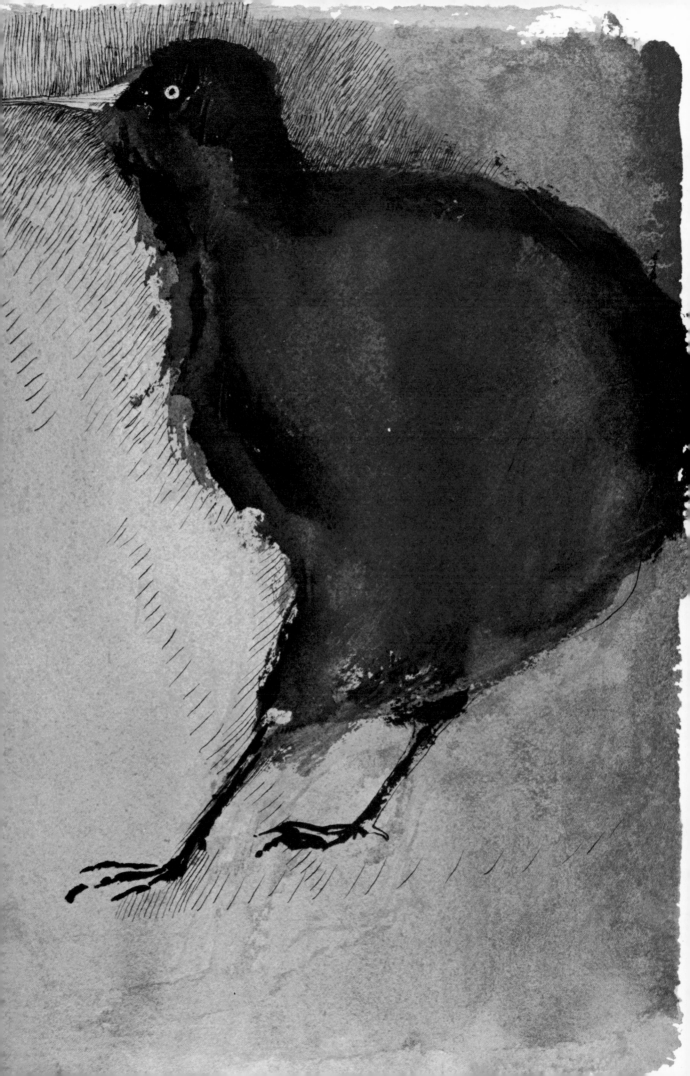

L

The omnivorous swarming locust

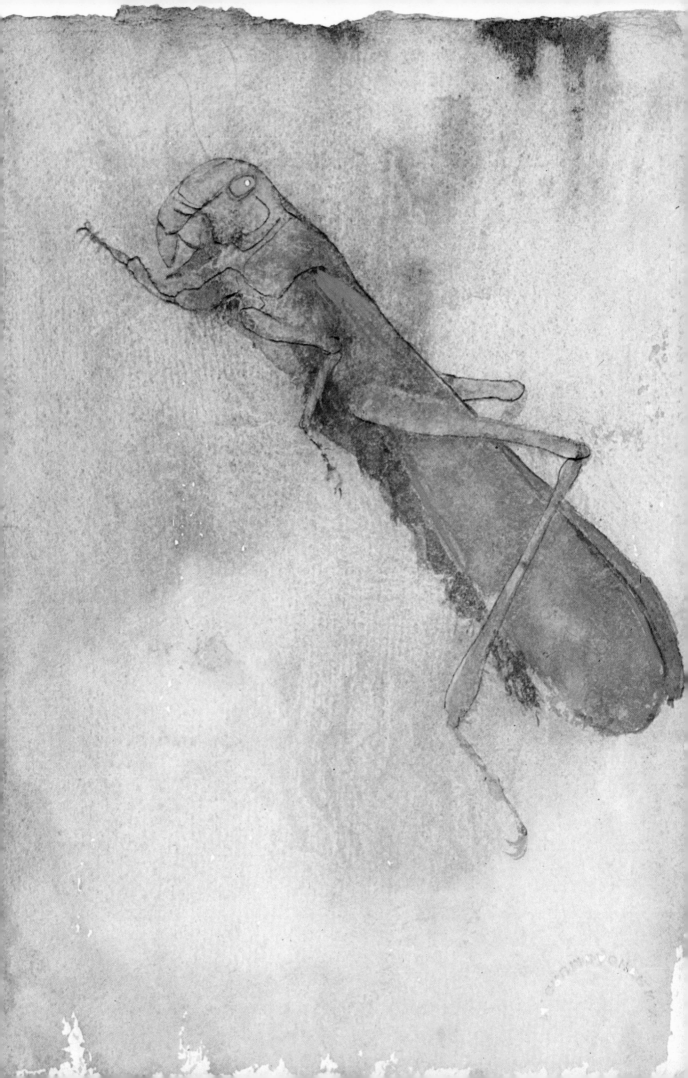

M   A mole in a hole

N

The

sweet-throated

nightingale

at

dusk

The eight-tentacled octopus

P   A primordial protozoa

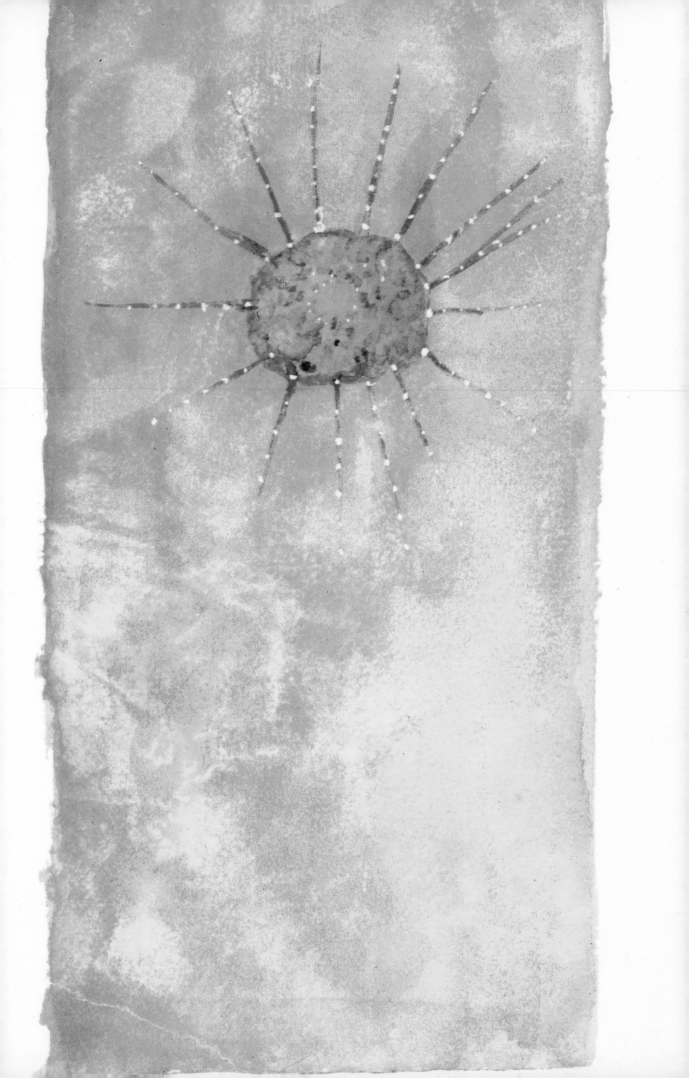

The quintessential quail

R

The

rhinoceros

express

S A
gangling
entangling
spider

T   A Scholastic Toad

U

The invisible unicorn

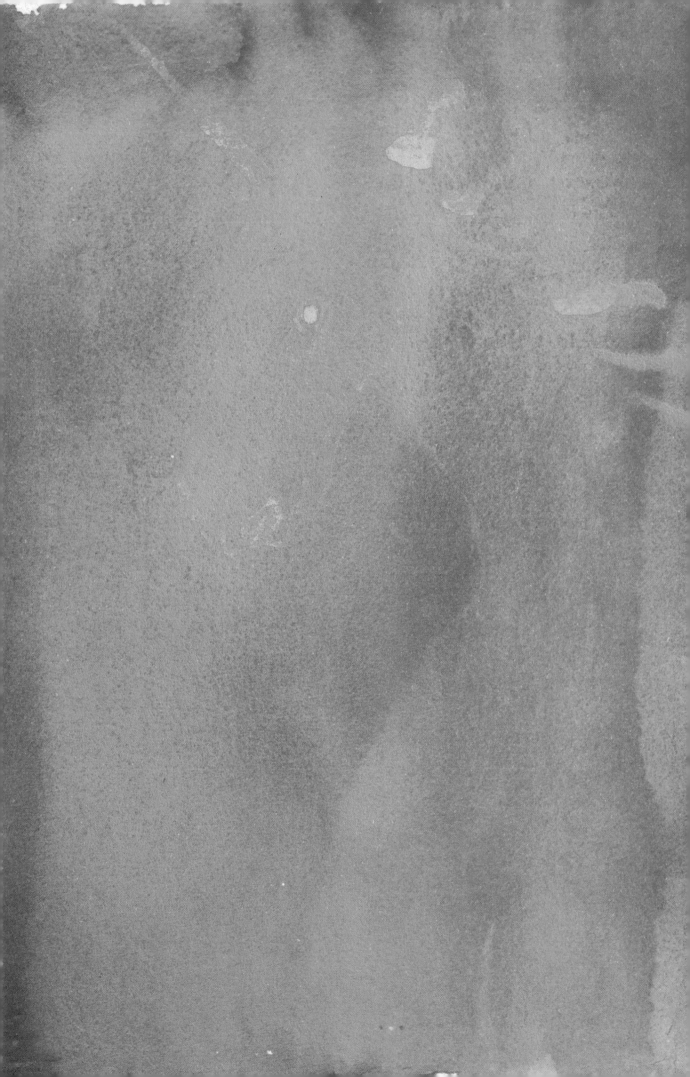

V
The cadaver-haunted vulture

W *whale, the*

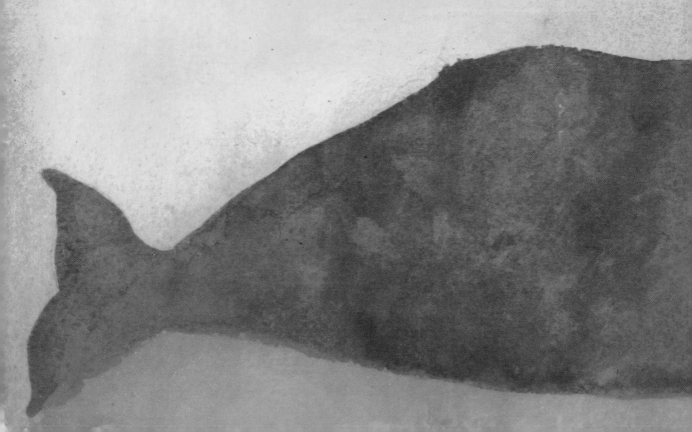

monster of the deep

X

The dragon of the alphabet

Y

The
double-breasted
yellow jacket

Z *A ruminating zebu*